WELSH RAILWAYS
- a new perspective

by

Jeff Morgan & Wayne Eldridge

INTRODUCTION

The photographs in this book cover a period of some thirty years from the early 1980s to the present. This has been a time of great change for the railways of Wales. In the mid-1980s the nationalised British Rail was privatised and since then there has been a large number of different companies, both passenger and freight, which have operated in the Principality.

The steep decline in, and final extinction of, deep mining has led to a severe drop in the number of coal trains operated. This has partially been offset, in South Wales, by the development of opencast mining and flows of imported coal. Similarly, the rationalisation of the metals industry, with, for example, the closure of Ebbw Vale, Velindre and Anglesey Aluminium works, together with the end of steel making at Llanwern has led to massive changes in freight volumes and operating patterns. In addition, restructuring of other industries and the loss of traffic to road haulage has led to the closure of a number of freight only branches. Lines closed during this period have included those to Amlwch in the north and Cynheidre, Maerdy and Trecwn in the south to name only a few amongst many.

On the other hand, passenger traffic has boomed, with many places having a better rail service than at any other time in their history. Over 40 stations in Wales have opened in the past thirty years including branches to Aberdare, Maesteg and Ebbw Vale. Many of these are re-openings to passenger traffic of stations and branches closed during the Beeching era. On the City Line in Cardiff, services have been introduced over a line that never carried any regular passenger trains! The number of passenger journeys in Wales rose from approximately 16.4 million in 1992-93 to 21.8 million in 2006-07. There are proposals for further developments in passenger traffic which will be very interesting to observe.

The aim of this book is to illustrate the ever-changing scene on the railways of Wales. It takes the form of a journey starting in the north west at Holyhead and finishing in the south west in Pembrokeshire. En route we will visit main lines and many branch lines of Wales. Wherever possible we have tried to show unusual, rare or long gone aspects of the Welsh railway scene. We have also tried to show photographs of less well-known locations, although many familiar ones are there as well. Inevitably, because of the density of the traffic and complexity of the system in South Wales, some three-quarters of the photographs are taken in that area. Since the closures of the Beeching era it has been impossible to travel directly by rail from North to South Wales without travelling through England, so a few of the photographs are located on the Marches Line.

Jeff and Wayne met as pupils at Pontypridd Boys' Grammar School in the early 1960s and have maintained their friendship and interest in railways ever since. From the early 1980s when Wayne returned to South Wales after time spent in Hertfordshire they have concentrated on recording the ever-changing scene in Wales. In that time they have built up a very large collection of their own photographs and have amassed a considerable library of reference materials on Welsh railways.

Rhagarweiniad

Dros y tri degawd a fu, teithiodd Jeff a Wayne o gwmpas Cymru yn cofnodi, drwy luniau, rheilffyrdd ein gwlad. Yn ystod y casgliad hwn, sydd yn cychwyn yn Sir Fôn, fe fyddwch yn cael eich cludo i'r De, efo'r daith yn terfynu yn Sir Benfro. Mae'r ddau hen gyfaill yn hyderus y byddwch chwithau hefyd yn mwynhau y daith ac yn cael eich diddanu wrth edrych ar y lluniau.

Acknowledgements

We would like to express our deep gratitude to Brian Mills and Rowland Pittard who have helped us enormously by providing us with information and clarifying facts. They also gave us a great deal of encouragement and used their expertise in checking our work. Thanks are also due to Nick Weedon and Austin Jeffery for help with the identification of various DMUs, to John Jones (Mold) for information and to Stuart Broad for technical assistance.

We would also like to thank Bernard McCall for his help and guidance during the production of this book and Lesley Bennett for her interest and support for the project. Finally we wish to thank our wives Edna and Jan for their encouragement during the production of this book. Additional thanks are due to Edna for providing the Welsh language introduction.

Jeff Morgan and Wayne Eldridge   *Cardiff*   *August, 2010*

Published by Bernard McCall, 400 Nore Road, Portishead, Bristol, BS20 8EZ, England. Website : www.coastalshipping.co.uk. Telephone/fax : 01275 846178. E-mail : bernard@coastalshipping.co.uk All distribution enquiries should be addressed to the publisher.

Printed by Amadeus Press, Ezra House, West 26 Business Park, Cleckheaton, West Yorkshire, BD19 4TQ. Telephone : 01274 863210; fax : 01274 863211. E-mail : info@amadeuspress.co.uk; website : www.amadeuspress.co.uk

ISBN : 978-1-902953-48-9

Front cover: On the fine morning of Wednesday 27 May 1992, 47 328 heads south through the beautiful countryside of the island of Anglesey with a train from the Associated Octel works at Amlwch. It is travelling towards the junction with the North Wales coast main line at Gaerwen. The load is ethylene dibromide and therefore for safety reasons there are barrier wagons next to the locomotive and brake van. The train will be staged at Llandudno Junction for several hours until leaving for its final destination at Ellesmere Port later in the afternoon. The Anglesey Central Railway opened to Amlwch in June 1867 and closed to passenger traffic in 1964. The line remained in use solely to carry the traffic from the Octel Works until its final closure in 1993, although the track has remained in situ, albeit heavily overgrown ever since.

Back cover: 37 425 and 37 419 head north towards Rhymney on Sunday 11 July 2004, through typical South Wales valley housing, having just left Tir Phil station. Double-heading of trains on the Rhymney Valley line was rare in regular service. However, on Sunday afternoons the empty stock train from Cardiff Canton depot to Rhymney was sometimes double-headed, occasionally running as a timetabled passenger train instead of the usual diesel unit. The locos and stock were returning after servicing, ready to form the Monday morning commuter trains to Cardiff.

Nearing the end of its 263 mile journey from London Euston, green-liveried D1648/47 851 reaches the bottom of the 1 in 75 gradient down into Holyhead station on Monday 23 August 2004. The working, operated by Virgin Trains, has just passed Holyhead signal box, which, with its 100 levers, was opened in 1937 and works 'absolute block' to Gaerwen signal box. Passengers on the train will be able, if they wish, to connect with the ferry to Dun Laoghaire in Ireland. At a higher level behind the locomotive can be seen the servicing shed and refuelling point, which is on the site of the old Holyhead steam depot.

In the early 1990s there was a plan by an enthusiast group in North Wales to restore passenger traffic on the Amlwch branch. In the early summer of 1992, Isle of Anglesey Railways Ltd/Rheilffyrdd Ynys Môn Cyf, operated trains over the line at weekends. These started and finished in Bangor. The trains ran under the title 'Lein Amlwch' and on Sunday 24 May 1992, unit L275, based at Longsight depot, Manchester is seen south of Llangefni. The company ran two trains a day and the train shown left Amlwch at 17.14 and was due to arrive at Bangor at 18.32. Since that year no further passenger trains have operated and following its closure to freight traffic in 1993, the track, while still in situ, has become very overgrown. Many attempts to re-open the line have not met with success; however, the Welsh Assembly Government has now commissioned a feasibility study on the reopening of the line as far as Llangefni.

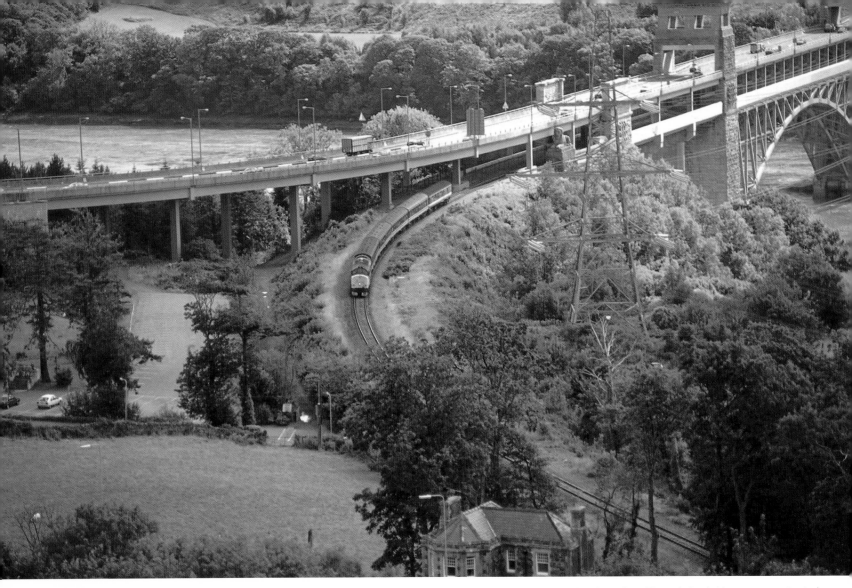

On the Anglesey side of the Menai Straits, close to the village of Llanfairpwll, stands the statue erected as a tribute to the Marquess of Anglesey, a hero of the Battle of Waterloo. From the top of the 27 metre high column on which the statue stands, a magnificent view can be obtained of the Menai Straits and the mountains of Snowdonia beyond. In this view taken from the vantage point on Monday 23 August 1993, 37 421 comes off Robert Stephenson's Menai Bridge with the 09.50 Manchester Victoria to Holyhead service. The tubular bridge was constructed between 1846 and 1850 and stood for 120 years before the tubes were destroyed by fire on 23 May 1970. After a complete reconstruction, it was reopened as a combined road and rail bridge in January 1972, with only the end towers remaining from the original bridge.

Conwy Castle is one of the series of castles erected by King Edward I in the 13th century, after his conquest of North Wales. This magnificent building forms the background to loco 37 421 as it brings a train from the Bangor direction into Llandudno Junction on Friday 15 April 1994. Below the train and close to the River Conwy can be seen tank and ballast wagons on the short branch which led down to Conwy Quay. The area in the foreground of the picture is now completely built over and this view can no longer be obtained. At Llandudno Junction, passengers could change for trains to Llandudno itself, a few miles to the north or for the 27-mile branch south to Blaenau Ffestiniog.

As travellers drop down into Blaenau Ffestiniog when heading south along the main A470 road, they are met by a virtual moonscape of slate waste left after more than 200 years of slate mining and quarrying. In this view taken in the early 1980s, a Llandudno Junction to Blaenau Ffestiniog train is travelling through the remains of the slate workings as it heads into the town. It has just passed through the 3,726 yard tunnel which is off the picture to the right. The present Blaenau station was opened in March 1982, to replace the original one at the northern edge of the town and is jointly operated with the narrow gauge Ffestiniog Railway. A few years ago a trial took place as part of a scheme to remove much of the waste by rail, but this has not yet come to fruition.

37 098 (leading) and 37 377 double-head the 'Roman Nose' excursion from London as it returns northwards into Blaenau Ffestiniog after traversing the Trawsfynydd branch on Saturday 18 April 1998. At the rear of the train was 59 205 *L Keith McNair*. This was the penultimate train over the branch after the closure of the nuclear power station at Trawsfynydd. The last train of all was run in atrocious weather on 17 October 1998. The section of the line on which the train is travelling was originally built in 1868 as a 1' 11¼" narrow gauge line for the Ffestiniog and Blaenau Railway. It was taken over by the GWR and converted to standard gauge in 1883 when the stone viaduct at the bottom of the picture replaced an earlier wooden one.

A large logo class 47 hurries a Holyhead to Euston train towards Abergele & Pensarn station at some time in the 1980s. The train is signalled through the eastbound centre line which was removed quite a few years ago. The signal gantry on the right still exists, but is now devoid of any signals although semaphore signals are still used at this location. Just 1³/₄ miles to the west of this spot was the site of the Abergele accident of August 1867 when the 'Irish Mail' ran into some runaway wagons which had been left on the main at Llanddulas during shunting operations. 32 people were killed in one of the worst railway accidents ever to occur in Wales.

On the morning of Saturday 10 August 2002, 47 292 in Freightliner livery, passes the site of Mold Junction at Saltney Ferry 3$^1/_2$ miles west of Chester station and close to the border with England. The train is an excursion from Llandudno Junction heading for the Settle to Carlisle line. At Mold Junction the former LNWR line to Mold and Denbigh branched off the North Wales coastline and headed away to the left of the picture. The former steam locomotive depot still stands behind the trees on the left and is now in use as a scrap yard. In the distance behind the train can be seen the new West Factory being constructed for Airbus Industries at Broughton. This factory, which opened on 4 July 2003, builds the wings for the A380 aircraft.

One of the last freight operations on the North Wales coast line is the movement of stone for ballast and other purposes from the quarry at Penmaenmawr. On Tuesday 24 August 2004, Freightliner-owned 66 506 *Crewe Regeneration* heads eastwards through Rhyl with a Penmaenmawr to Crewe ballast train made up of JNA wagons. The train is passing the former Rhyl No. 2 signal box, built by the London and North Western Railway in 1900 and containing 126 levers. Although closed, as a listed structure it cannot be demolished but unfortunately a suitable use has yet to be found for it. The station is now signalled by the remaining No.1 box situated at the opposite end of the same platform.

Dee Marsh exchange sidings serve Shotton steelworks which is still a busy industrial complex in north-east Wales. Trains heading to the north west of England have to travel south to Wrexham where they run round at Croes Newydd before heading north. Having performed this manoeuvre, 56 062 heads a Dee Marsh to Warrington steel train at Balderton Crossing on Tuesday 7 August 2002. The ex-Great Western Railway main line from Wrexham General station north towards Chester was singled in 1986. There are plans for re-doubling this section because of serious delays caused by the growth of passenger traffic over the line in recent years.

Chester is a major nodal point for rail traffic in the North West. From here, trains travel to Holyhead, Wrexham, Crewe, Warrington and Birkenhead. The station was opened in 1848 as part of the Chester & Holyhead Railway and still remains an extremely busy place over 160 years later. In this photograph, taken in the 1980s, a class 46 awaits departure on an eastbound train while two Met-Cam class 101 DMUs stand at the adjacent platform. Modern developments have changed the layout considerably at this station, but it still remains a fascinating example of traditional station architecture. Further redevelopment of the station is planned for 2010.

On Tuesday 3 August 1982, 20 178 & 20 182 double-head a train of Presflo wagons from the cement works at Padeswood through Cefn-y-Bedd towards Wrexham. This line was built by the Wrexham, Mold and Connah's Quay Railway in 1866 and was later part of the Great Central. After the grouping it became the only section of the London & North Eastern Railway in Wales. Today a regular interval service of passenger trains operates from Wrexham Central to Bidston along this line. It is also used for regular steel trains between South Wales and Shotton steel works.

In April 1986, the colliery at Bersham, just south of Wrexham, was still in production. One of the original class 150 DMUs is passing the site on a Chester to Shrewsbury via Wrexham working. Just a few months later in December 1986, the colliery closed. When the site was cleared, one set of winding gear was left and can still be seen, one of the very few sets of winding gear left in Wales. The train is passing Bersham signal box which controlled access to the complex and closed two months after rail traffic ceased at the colliery.

A busy moment at Gobowen on Monday 28 July 2003 as 60 081 *Isambard Kingdom Brunel* brings a Llanwern – Dee Marsh steel train north. On the right, 66 074 stands on the erstwhile Oswestry branch waiting to follow with an empty timber train. This has come south from the Kronospan chipboard factory at Chirk in order to run round on the stub of the branch before heading back north. On the right are HEA wagons carrying house coal for local distribution. They are awaiting unloading at Smallshaws coal depot, at that time one of the last operational railway coal depots in the country. The Oswestry branch is still intact but greatly overgrown and is the subject of a fledgling heritage operation, but the Smallshaws depot has now closed.

Machynlleth is the operational hub for the whole former Cambrian Railways system. In this photograph taken in the 1980s, a class 37 hauled train leaves the station in the Shrewsbury direction whilst a class 150 unit waits alongside the depot. Machynlleth signal box was built in 1960 to replace the former East and West boxes and operates the only semaphore signals on the Cambrian system (except those used to control level crossings at a few locations). At present the Cambrian system uses the Radio Electronic Token Block signalling system (RETB), but is soon to adopt the European Rail Traffic Management System (ERTMS).

With the waters of Cardigan Bay in the background, two Met-Cam 101 DMUs cross at Tywyn. The train on the left is heading north to Pwllheli while the one on the right is heading south towards Machynlleth. The signal box, which was built by the Great Western Railway in 1923, closed in 1988 but the loop remains and is a token exchange point. At the time the photograph was taken in the early 1980s, the coal yard was still open. However, these days, the whole of the Cambrian system sees no regular freight traffic.

The driver of 37 431 *Sir Powys/County of Powys* waits for the level-crossing gates to descend before bringing his train across the road to Tremadog (A487) and into Porthmadog station with a train for Pwllheli on Saturday 29 July 1989. This Cambrian Railways station opened in 1867 and is still a crossing point on the line. Just visible on the left of the picture is the Porthmadog station of the 1' 11½" gauge Welsh Highland Heritage Railway.

No freight trains are scheduled over the Central Wales line, but on very rare occasions when there is engineering work elsewhere, trains use the line as a diversionary route. On Sunday 16 April 2006, because of work on a railway bridge at Bridgend, trains between Margam and Llanwern were diverted via Llandrindod Wells. At Craven Arms, locomotives ran round their trains then headed south again via Hereford. The photograph shows 66 189 working north through Knighton with slab steel from Margam to Llanwern, passing 66 149 on the right of the picture with a Llanwern to Margam empties. The loop at Knighton was lifted in 1965 and re-laid in 1990. It is interesting that at Knighton the station is in England whilst the town is in Wales.

In the days of steam, Llandeilo was the largest station between Swansea and Craven Arms. It is now a shadow of its former self but still retains its loop. This proved very useful on Sunday 23 April 2006 when it was used to cross two steel trains running between Llanwern and Margam which had been diverted due to engineering work on the South Wales main line. On the left of the picture, 66 089 stands with a southbound Llanwern to Margam empties train waiting for the arrival of 66 025 with a Margam to Llanwern slab train. The whole of the Central Wales line works under the No Signalman Key Token system which is supervised by Pantyffynnon signal box. This system was introduced in 1986.

On Wednesday 7 August 2002, 60 093 *Jack Stirk* has just reversed into sidings at the north end of Hereford station. The empty PGA wagons are to be filled with crushed stone in the old goods yard by means of a mechanical shovel. The train was booked to depart for Westbury at 14.00 that afternoon. This traffic was later transferred to a new purpose-built facility at Moreton-on-Lugg four miles to the north. 158 831 in the now defunct Alphaline livery passes with a southbound passenger working.

During the early years of the 21st century, a loco-hauled train was run in connection with the Royal Welsh show at Builth Wells. Trains were run to Builth Road station with a special bus connection to the showground at Llanelwedd. During the day the locomotive and stock were stabled at Llandrindod Wells. This photograph taken on Monday 19 July 2004, shows the driver looking back to check the train as 37 406 *The Saltire Society* leaves Ffairfach station with the return 17.45 Llandrindod Wells to Rhymney train and crosses the A483 main road through the town. The train on that day ran 35 minutes late from Llandovery because it was unable to cross a northbound train at Llandeilo as timetabled, due to damage to the points at the loop there. The former signal box at Ffairfach station has been preserved as a signalling & telegraph museum at the Gwili Railway near Carmarthen.

In spite of much investment in locomotives and infrastructure during the early years of the 21st century, the carriage of mail by rail in Britain had completely finished by January 2004. There has been some return of mail traffic to the railways, but not in the Wales and Marches area. On Monday 14 August 2000, 67 028 & 67 008 double-head a northbound empty mail train from Bristol Temple Meads (ex Barton Hill) to Warrington into Hereford past the former DMU stabling point at Edgar Street sidings.

During the 1990s, the large sawmills based near the village of Pontrilas on the Newport to Hereford line received some timber by rail. Railway wagons were unloaded at the site of the old station for onward movement by road the short distance to the mills. On Wednesday 23 October 1997, RES-liveried 47 760 backs its wagons into the siding in front of Pontrilas signal box. The 42-lever signal box was built by the GWR in 1880 and is still operational. The train was tripped from Newport Alexandra Dock Junction yard after arrival from West Wales.

Looking north from Chapel Lane bridge, 66 017 stands in Panteg down goods loop with a Dee Marsh to Llanwern/Margam train on Saturday 13 September 2008, while a class 175/1 unit heads from the Pontypool & New Inn direction towards Newport. The siding on the right was installed many years ago in anticipation of traffic to and from the Pilkington Brothers fibreglass factory which is hidden behind the high hedge on the right. However, it is extremely doubtful that it has ever carried any traffic.

In recent years the autumn leaf-fall season has caused major problems on the track, with trains losing traction and/or unable to stop effectively, often damaging wheel tyres. This can be due to the combination of damp and crushed leaves on the railhead. To counter this, special trains are run which water jet the railhead and put down a paste which helps the wheel/railhead contact area. Here, 37 419 and 37 698 are seen at Maindee North Junction at Newport on the line from Abergavenny having just passed under the M4 motorway with a railhead treatment train. This photograph was taken on Saturday 9 October 2004.

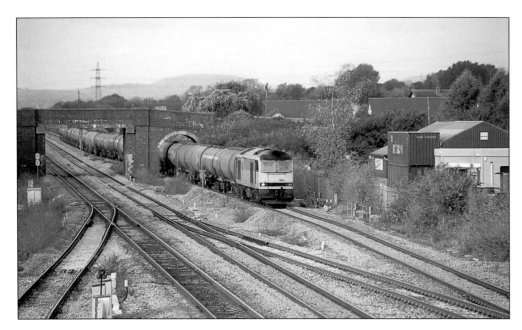

The main line between Cardiff and Severn Tunnel Junction consists of four tracks. The original two track line was extended to four tracks by the Great Western Railway in 1941. Evidence of this can be seen where the original road bridge has obviously been widened at a later date. In the immediate foreground is the site of the former Magor station which closed in November 1964. Having crossed over the Bishton Flyover approximately one mile behind the train, 60 066 is travelling on the up relief line towards Severn Tunnel Junction with the morning oil train from the Murco refinery at Robeston to Westerleigh on Friday 2 November 2007.

Some of the coal now used in South Wales at places such as Aberthaw power station, is brought into Britain through Portbury or Avonmouth. On Monday 19 February 2007, 66 099 is on the down relief line at Llanwern Works West Connection with HTA wagons bound for Aberthaw. To the right of the picture, 09 017 waits for a clear road with a transfer train from Llanwern steelworks to Newport Docks. The steelworks, now much reduced in size over recent years, lies behind the trees. Until recently this was one of the few locations that class 09 shunting locomotives hauled trains on the main line, but this practice has now ceased.

Until the early years of the 21st century, the massive steelworks at Llanwern to the east of Newport was a major centre for freight traffic in South Wales. The iron ore used in the blast furnaces was imported through the docks at Port Talbot and taken by rail to Llanwern. These trains were amongst the heaviest ever to run in Britain. On Bank Holiday Monday 28 May 2000, 60 035 *Florence Nightingale* heads the empty iron ore tippler wagons towards the camera and passes 60 048 *Saddleback* with the full wagons from Port Talbot. The blast furnaces at Llanwern closed and the iron ore traffic ceased in 2001. The heavy end of the steelworks was subsequently demolished and all the buildings seen in the background of this photograph have now disappeared.

The 3-mile-long Uskmouth branch leaves the main line at East Usk yard at Newport. One siding on the branch in use in the early part of the 21st century was adjacent to the Orb steelworks. On Friday 4 June 2004, 37 698, in Loadhaul livery, is propelling its train down the branch. There were no run round facilities at the Orb works, so it was necessary to have a brake van at the front of the train manned by a lookout equipped with a radio and horn. Just to the right of the locomotive can be seen East Usk signal box which opened in April 1961 as part of the Newport MAS scheme. It controlled only the junction for the branch and not the main lines. The original lower quadrant semaphores were replaced in recent years by upper quadrants, the only ones seen in South Wales at that time. The box was destroyed by fire on April 19 2009 and by March 2010 the semaphore signals had been dismantled.

The top of the multi-storey car park near the west bank of the River Usk at Newport provides an excellent view of rail traffic crossing the river bridge. On Tuesday 19 February 2002, 60 032 *William Booth* heads a Robeston – Westerleigh oil train on the up relief and passes 66 029 on the down relief with a westbound coal train of HTA wagons. In the 1960s the refineries at Milford Haven despatched a large number of oil trains, but closures and pipeline use has reduced this considerably in recent years. To the right of the picture is Maindee West Junction with the lines curving off to Abergavenny and Hereford.

Hillfield Tunnel which lies to the immediate west of Newport station was built in 1850. In 1912 the Great Western Railway widened the line between Newport and Cardiff to four tracks which meant a new bore had to be constructed alongside the original one. Topographical features meant that at its eastern end this tunnel was 22 yards longer than the earlier one. In this photograph, taken on Thursday 20 April 2006, 66 101 emerges from the original 1850s tunnel on what is now the up relief line with an engineering train of empty JNA wagons. At the same time an HST in First Great Western livery comes out of the 1912 tunnel with a Paddington bound train and slows for its stop at Newport station. The engineering sidings on the left of the picture were lifted in 2009.

One train on two branches! On Saturday 19 April 1997, the 'Welsh Wizard' rail tour visited lines in South Wales. In this photograph, 37 254 (nearest the camera) at the head of the train, is taking the former Dock Street branch at Waterloo Loop Junction, Newport, while at the rear of the train 37 230 is just coming off the Newport Docks branch. The train will travel down the branch to its end at Courtybella unloading site. On its return to Alexandra Dock Junction Yard, visible in the distance alongside the main line, the two class 37s were replaced by 56 044 *Cardiff Canton* and 56 118 for the journey to Barry Docks and Cwmbargoed.

The Monmouthshire Railway Society was well-known in the latter years of the 20th century, for its railtours over freight-only lines in South Wales, many of which were due for closure at the time. On Saturday 5 April 1986, the Risca Cuckoo tour led by driving coach W51353, crosses the busy Commercial Street in Newport, heading for Dock Street Yard. At that time this was the site of a house coal distribution depot. The level crossing gates are not in the best of health and the train is being flagged across the road whilst lines of traffic wait for its passing.

The recently-constructed southern bypass road for Newport has opened up some new photographic opportunities where it crosses the lines to the docks. On Saturday 4 February 2006, 66 007 headed south on the west side of Newport Docks, bringing a train of loaded coal from the opencast site at Parc Slip near Tondu. This coal will be unloaded by mechanical grab just a few yards beyond this point, at a newly-constructed pad and then transported the short distance by road to South Dock. Here it will be blended with imported coal and the blend carried by rail to Uskmouth power station.

For many years the Ebbw Vale steelworks at the top of the Western Valleys line from Newport, received and sent out much traffic by rail. In this photograph, taken on Friday 23 February 2001, 60 053 *Nordic Terminal* passes the site of Llanhilleth station with a short train of steel coil bound for the works. The train has come from Margam and has taken the Cardiff Curve at Newport to access the branch. At the works, the steel will be coated with tin for various industrial uses. Prominent in the background of the photograph is the Llanhilleth Miners' Institute opened in 1906. Many institutes which were once a common sight in the valleys of South Wales have been demolished or lie derelict. However, this one has now been restored to use as a centre of community life.

With typical valleys housing in the background and foreground, a Monmouthshire Railway Society tour, the 'Risca Cuckoo' is photographed near Abertillery as it heads towards the recently closed Rose Heyworth Colliery on the branch which left the main Western Valleys line at Aberbeeg. The line originally ran through to Brynmawr but had been cut back to Rose Heyworth for many years. The date is Saturday 5 April 1986 and the train made up of class 116 and 117 DMUs was thought at the time to be the last one which would ever traverse this branch. However, there are now proposals to reopen the section from Aberbeeg to Abertillery to passenger traffic as part of Phase 2 of the Western Valleys re-opening scheme. Earlier on its journey the train had passed through the town of Risca. The tour's name 'Risca Cuckoo' comes from a local legend about some men who tried to trap a cuckoo in their garden by building ever higher hedges around the bird's nest. Another photograph of the tour is on page 23.

The closure of the steelworks at Ebbw Vale was announced on 1 February 2001. The last production took place on 1 June of the same year and by July 2002 demolition had started on site. On Monday 29 July 2002, 66 154 waits to leave Ebbw Vale South Yard with a train of SSA wagons bound for Tidal Sidings, Cardiff. These contained some of the rollers from the rolling mills used for rolling steel coil into thinner sections. In the background it can be seen that work has already started on lifting the track of the South Yard.

After the closure of Ebbw Vale steelworks the Western Valleys line remained dormant for several years. However, in 2008 it re-opened to passenger traffic after a period of track refurbishment or realignment and the building of new stations. Most stations on the line opened with the new service on 6 February 2008. One of the stations which did not open on this date was at Llanhilleth. On Saturday 16 February 2008, a four-car set made up of two class 150 units on an Ebbw Vale Parkway – Cardiff working, passes the site of the new Llanhilleth station where construction work is still continuing. The station opened on Sunday 25 April 2008. Passenger traffic on the Ebbw Vale branch has exceeded all predictions. At present all trains run direct to Cardiff but it is hoped that Newport station will be served in the near future.

The Hanson quarry east of Machen has provided vast tonnages of crushed stone for various uses including railway ballast. It stands on the former Brecon and Merthyr Railway on what is now the end of a 6-mile branch line from Park Junction on the Ebbw Vale line. Originally the line continued to Bargoed and Rhymney. On Friday 5 April 2002, 66 068 stands at the outlet road from the quarry with loaded ballast wagons for the short journey to Newport Alexandra Dock Junction Yard. In the distance on the right of the train can be seen the quarry shunting locomotive class 03 D2199 which was on loan to Hanson Aggregates and is owned by the Heritage Shunters Trust.

A very unusual event took place on Saturday 27 March 2004 when 47 843 expired with low oil pressure at Abergavenny on the 09.13 train from Crewe en route to Cardiff Central. The train was carrying supporters for the Wales v Italy rugby game at the Millennium Stadium. Following behind on the 09.50 Crewe – Cardiff was 47 845 (D1733), also carrying supporters. This train coupled up behind the failed train and propelled it all the way to Cardiff where it arrived some time after the start of the game. The photograph shows the two trains passing Newport Alexandra Dock Junction Yard.

The closure of Wembley Stadium in London in 2002, meant that many of the football games usually played there were transferred to the Millennium Stadium in Cardiff which had opened in June 1999. This in turn, led to an increased number of locomotive hauled special trains into Cardiff. On Saturday 22 May 2004, 47 847 speeds west along the main line between Cardiff and Newport with a train of football supporters from Manchester.

They are going to see the F A Cup Final between Manchester United and Millwall which Manchester United won 3-0. The train is passing 60 091 *An Teallach*, which is travelling on the down relief line with empty oil tanks for the Murco refinery at Robeston.

On most evenings, the Freightliner terminal at Pengam on the eastern outskirts of Cardiff was a very busy place. The Rover Way overbridge provided an ideal vantage point for photography. On Wednesday 10 June 1998, 37 609, 20 306 and 20 310 in DRS livery, prepare to triple-head the 18.20 Freightliner to Coatbridge (Glasgow). The train will have to run up the branch towards Tidal Sidings which lies behind the camera, before running round and proceeding eastwards away from the camera. Just visible is a class 47 locomotive waiting to take another Freightliner train. In 1999, Pengam Freightliner terminal closed and was relocated some three miles east at Wentloog. The entire Freightliner site at Pengam is now a housing estate.

On Saturday 24 September 1994, the Branch Line Society ran a tour in South Wales which covered several lines along the coastal strip, including Barry Docks, Aberthaw power station and the Baglan Bay branch. The tour was called 'The Port Vale' because it visited the ports of Cardiff and Barry and the Vale of Glamorgan. It is seen here in the sidings at the Castle Works of Allied Steel & Wire just south of Long Dyke Junction in Cardiff. At the head of the train stands 37 429 Eisteddfod Genedlaethol in Regional Railways livery, while at the rear of the train 37 158 in engineering 'Dutch' livery, can just be seen. The works is still operational but is now owned by Celsa.

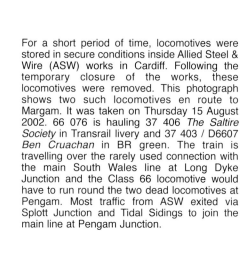

For a short period of time, locomotives were stored in secure conditions inside Allied Steel & Wire (ASW) works in Cardiff. Following the temporary closure of the works, these locomotives were removed. This photograph shows two such locomotives en route to Margam. It was taken on Thursday 15 August 2002. 66 076 is hauling 37 406 The Saltire Society in Transrail livery and 37 403 / D6607 Ben Cruachan in BR green. The train is travelling over the rarely used connection with the main South Wales line at Long Dyke Junction and the Class 66 locomotive would have to run round the two dead locomotives at Pengam. Most traffic from ASW exited via Splott Junction and Tidal Sidings to join the main line at Pengam Junction.

The first dock in Cardiff was opened in 1839 and for the next 70 years there was continuous development of the dock system. The final dock in Cardiff was the Queen Alexandra Dock, opened in 1912. The north side of this dock was developed for general cargoes rather than the coal exports to be found in the other docks. It is here that 08 352 is standing on Friday 16 April 1982. The locomotive has just brought down a train of steel coil from the Allied Steel & Wire works to the north of the dock system. The coil is being loaded aboard the Greek-flagged vessel *Eleni D* for onward shipment. The ship was built in Japan in 1969. The Queen Alexandra Dock is still in commercial use but all the quayside lines are now closed.

Crossing over from the down relief line to the down main, to run through the middle roads at Cardiff Central Station, is 37 899. It is on a train of empty MDV wagons from Newport Docks, heading towards Maesteg to load stockpiled coal. The train is coming up the 1 in 47 gradient from Newtown West. To the right, tracks lead up and around to the left and into Queen Street Station. The date is August 1989 and since then, the cityscape of Cardiff as seen in the background has changed out of all recognition, with many of the buildings being demolished and replaced.

At 18.15 on the sunny evening of Thursday 4 May 1995, 37 875 leads two sister locomotives through Heath Junction as they triple-head a loaded coal train from Cwmbargoed to Aberthaw. For a short period of time, triple-heading was fairly normal on these trains in order to provide sufficient braking power on the long downhill gradients from Cwmbargoed. At Heath Junction the short 2$^1/_2$ mile commuter branch to Coryton leaves the Rhymney line. The locomotives are passing the site of the original junction which was re-laid on 19 November 1984, a few hundred yards to the north. At the same time, Heath Junction signal box was replaced by a new portakabin type building which is hidden from view by the train.

Some of the last locomotive-hauled commuter trains in Wales operated in the Rhymney Valley. At one point, three such trains ran down to Cardiff from Rhymney in the morning and returned in the evening. A wide variety of locomotives was used at various times, including classes 33, 37, 47 and 50. However, on only one occasion was a class 56 locomotive used on a Rhymney to Cardiff train.

Following the failure due to low coolant of 37 402, it was replaced by 56 114 on Tuesday 8 April 2003. This was a great surprise because class 56 locomotives were not allowed into Rhymney due to weight restrictions. The photograph shows the loco arriving at Heath High Level at 08.15 on that day.

Llanishen Station was opened by the Rhymney Railway in 1871 when they completed the line south from Caerphilly through the 1 mile 181 yard Caerphilly Tunnel, down to Cardiff. In 1999 the Rugby World Cup was held in the new Millennium Stadium in Cardiff. On Saturday 9 October in that year 31 602 *Chimaera* and 31 601 *Bletchley Park - Station X* double-head a rugby special north into Llanishen. The train is carrying happy Welsh supporters who have just seen Wales defeat Japan 64-15. Double-heading of trains on rugby days was extremely rare since if a second locomotive was allocated to the train, they usually worked in top and tail formation.

Regular freight traffic on the Rhymney line consists mainly of coal and until recently, infrequent stone traffic. A welcome change to this is the rare passage of military vehicles in connection with army manoeuvres in the Sennybridge area of the Brecon Beacons. Vehicles are transported by rail from various army depots to Cwmbargoed for onward transport by road. On Tuesday 25 June 2002, 66 138 brings its loaded train of Warwell and Warflat wagons south through Caerphilly with its load from Cwmbargoed. Caerphilly is by far the busiest station on the Rhymney line and still retains a manned booking office for most of the day.

Until the early 1990s, the lines around Nelson and Treharris continued to be busy with coal traffic. Three mines were open in the area, Trelewis Drift, Taff Merthyr Colliery and Deep Navigation Colliery. Waste shale from the collieries was transported by rail to the delightfully named 'Nelson Bog' where it was unloaded and transferred further up the mountain by road. This facility was opened in 1977. On Friday 20 April 1990, 37 692 stands at the Nelson Bog unloading site, while 37 801 *Aberthaw / Aberddawan* passes with a loaded coal train heading towards the junction with the Rhymney Valley line at Ystrad Mynach. The loaded train is travelling on what was once the Pontypool Road to Neath line, but will soon curve round to the right and drop down to Ystrad Mynach via the single line Penallta (or Penalltau) branch. This was not the line to Penallta Colliery which was situated on the Cylla branch from Ystrad Mynach. The last of the three collieries in this area, Taff Merthyr, closed in 1993.

The use of class 58 locomotives on trains in the South Wales valleys was virtually unheard of until the late 1990s. However, around that time they started being used on trains from Westbury to Cwmbargoed which returned with locally-quarried stone. On Friday 29 May 1998, 58 014 *Didcot Power Station* in Mainline livery, heads empty wagons through the site of Bedlinog station on the long climb to Cwmbargoed. The old Station Hotel is closed and boarded up, but has since been renovated as a commercial property, but alas not as a pub.

The long climb up from the Rhymney valley to Cwmbargoed provided ideal test bed conditions when work was carried out to check automatic uncoupling of banking locomotives which were to be used on the Lickey Incline. On Thursday 1 August 2002, the Cwmbargoed branch had been out of use for some time following the temporary end of opencast mining in the area. 66 041 arrives at the site with a test train and on the rear can be seen 66 250. The FHA wagon behind the rake of loaded HAA wagons is carrying the automatic test uncoupling monitoring equipment. Several runs were made during the day. These proved successful and the system is now in use on the Lickey Incline.

The Taff Vale Railway's workshops at Cathays in Cardiff remained in use until early in the 21st century. They carried out repairs to a wide range of rolling stock, including infrastructure wagons and track maintenance equipment. Many different types of wagons can be seen in this photograph which was taken in June 1992 and is looking south in the direction of Queen Street station. In the distance, a class 08 shunter can be seen making up the return afternoon trip working to Radyr yard. The class 08 in the foreground was included in the trip working as a dead locomotive. In 1993 the yard was closed as a general workshop but remained in use by various railway companies in the privatisation era. The last company to make use of the site was Pullman Rail which moved its operations to Cardiff Canton at the end of 2005. Much of the site has since been redeveloped.

In August 1981, a class 37 on a loaded coal train waits to join the ex-Taff Vale line just to the north of Llandaff station. The train is standing on the Llandaff Loop which provided access from the southern end of Radyr marshalling yards for trains heading towards Cardiff Queen Street station and the western parts of South Wales. Part of the yard can be seen in the background to the right of the photograph as can Radyr Quarry Junction signal box. This just failed to reach its centenary having been built by the TVR in 1899 and closed on 12 May 1998. The bridge in the foreground carried the railway over the erstwhile Glamorganshire Canal and the land to the right is now occupied by housing.

The City Line between Radyr and Cardiff Central stations was opened on 4 October 1987. Strangely enough this ex-TVR line had never seen regular passenger trains before this date. Brand-new stations were opened at Danescourt, Fairwater and Waungron Park and the former football halt at Ninian Park was refurbished. In the months leading up to the opening, a morning Merthyr - Cardiff Central service, was routed via the line in order to continue on to Bristol Temple Meads. The photograph shows this train, a Valley Lines class 116 DMU, passing construction work on the new Danescourt station.

The visit of Pope John Paul II to Cardiff on Wednesday 2 June 1982 brought a very large number of special excursion trains to the city. Many of these trains were stabled in a part of Radyr Yard which had been specially cleared for the occasion. Other rakes of empty stock were stabled on the former relief lines between Taff's Well and Radyr. Special instructions were issued stating that the rakes must not be stabled adjacent to one another but had to be parked in a staggered formation. At 19.45 on the evening of that momentous day, 45 070 has collected empty stock from south of Taff's Well and stands on the relief line adjacent to the station at Radyr. It will run to Cardiff Central via Ninian Park and form the 20.15 return working to Retford. Radyr station was remodelled in 1999 and the signal box and semaphore signalling dismantled.

In the 1980s some of the South Wales collieries used ex-British Rail or hired in British Rail shunting locomotives for internal use. These locos were maintained at Cardiff Canton depot. On Friday 19 July 1985, a class 37 locomotive heads along the down relief line next to Radyr station. It is hauling three shunting locomotives to Canton. These are 08 896, D3183 and D3014; the latter two locomotives were at Merthyr Vale colliery and both returned there, D3183 in August 1986 and D3014 in March 1986. D3183 was cut up on site in December 1987, but D3014 has been preserved on the Paignton and Dartmouth Railway. The layout at Radyr was considerably altered in the 1990s and the relief lines abolished.

When the new colliery at Nantgarw was opened in the1950s a new rail connection to serve it was opened from the north end of Taff's Well station to join the ex-Cardiff Railway just south of the old Glan-y-Llyn station. The branch remained open until the closure of the Nantgarw complex in 1987. A few months before the closure, a F & W Railtour visited the branch and is seen on Saturday 11 October 1986 approaching the CWS (Co-operative Wholesale Society) level crossing at Taff's Well just before the junction with the ex-TVR main line. The train is being hauled by 37 697. Coincidentally, this locomotive was the last one ever to use the branch when on 30 September 1990 it hauled out a rake of stored wagons. It had been expected that these wagons would be cut up on site, but environmental considerations meant that the branch had to be re-opened for one last time to collect them. For a period after closure a short stub of the branch, as far as the CWS level crossing, was used for the reversal of DMUs from the Cardiff direction which terminated at Taff's Well.

The clock on St. Catherine's Church shows four o'clock in the afternoon on a warm summer's day in 1983, as 37 222 brings a loaded train of MDVs through the junction at Pontypridd. The coal is coming from a colliery in the Taff or Cynon Valleys. In Taff Vale Railway days, this was one of the busiest locations in the whole of the South Wales coalfield. The line up the Rhondda Valley to Porth diverges to the left. At Porth the Treherbert line continues up the Rhondda Fawr, while the mineral only line to Mardy Colliery branched up the Rhondda Fach until its closure in 1986. The brick building just seen on the left, is part of Pontypridd Junction signal box which was opened in 1902 and closed on 15 October 1998. It is now a grade II listed building.

The line south from Treherbert to Porth is single track with a passing loop at Ystrad Rhondda. Between Porth and Pontypridd, double track has been retained and the excessive width of the formation shows that there were originally four tracks at this point. It is on this latter section, just south of Porth, that Railtrack class 121 bubblecar 960011 was photographed on Sunday 15 June 2003. The unit was fitted with video surveying equipment and during that day, travelled over many of the valley lines checking the condition of track. The class 121 units were built in the early 1960s and are now one of the oldest types of vehicle in operation with Network Rail.

Just south of Abercynon is Stormstown yard. In the mid-1980s, a class 37 is hauling a train of HEA wagons heading for Abercwmboi on the Aberdare branch. At the same time, a double-headed train in the far distance comes off the Ynysybwl branch with coal from Lady Windsor colliery. The coal in a rake of MDV wagons in the yard is being manually trimmed. They have been loaded by the Ryan Company cranes in the sidings behind the signal gantry. These sidings originally led to Parc Newydd Colliery and were controlled by Carn Parc signal box which was situated in the immediate right foreground of the picture. The line to Ynysybwl was controlled by Stormstown signal box which was situated near to the junction itself. At the time of the photograph, the whole area was controlled by Abercynon signal box which is a few hundred yards behind the photographer.

The last working colliery in the upper Taff Valley was at Merthyr Vale. This photograph was taken on Tuesday 8 August 1989 just a few months before its closure. In the foreground a class 150 unit is travelling south from Merthyr Tydfil on the hourly passenger service to Cardiff. The line between Merthyr and Abercynon was single with a passing loop at Black Lion signal box. In the colliery yard below, 37 689 has just arrived with empty MGR wagons. The loco will run round and the train will be filled by mechanical shovels visible in the photograph. Due to the steep gradient between the colliery and the main line, the filled train will be run in two sections to Black Lion sidings before being reunited for its onward run to Abercwmboi Phurnacite plant. The loop and sidings together with the signal box were taken out of use in 1992. A new loop at the reconstructed Merthyr Vale station was opened in 2009 as part of the upgrading of passenger services to Merthyr Tydfil.

A 'Hoover' passes the Hoover factory! The class 50 locomotives are often referred to as 'Hoovers' by enthusiasts, due to their distinctive engine sound. This photograph was taken on Sunday 16 August 1998 and shows 50 031 *Hood* on a special train passing the factory at Pentrebach just south of Merthyr Tydfil. It is approaching the site of the former Brandy Bridge Junction where the GWR line to Merthyr High Street station left the original TVR line into Merthyr. During the day the train also visited the Rhondda Valley. The Hoover factory closed on 13 March 2009 after some sixty years of production.

The morning of Monday 20 December 1999 was cold and snowy. In such weather 66 138 arrives at the loading pad for Tower Colliery with empty wagons. This was the first train up since the snow fell, as can be seen by the state of the track in front of the locomotive. The driver is receiving run-round instructions from the shunter. Tower Colliery was closed by British Coal on 22 April 1994 and was subject to a management buyout. The new company known as Tower-Goitre Anthracite Ltd, reopened the colliery in October 1994. For fourteen years production continued until final closure in January 2008 due to depleted reserves. However, the loading pad continues in use for a weekly train of the output from opencast and drift mines. Until February 2010, occasional stone traffic from a local quarry was also loaded here.

Between Tower colliery at Hirwaun and Cwmbach, trains use the old GWR Pontypool Road – Neath line before crossing the valley to join the original TVR line. Just south of Robertstown Crossing 56 053 *County of Mid-Glamorgan / Sir Morgannwg Ganol* is pictured on Tuesday 9 August with a loaded 'merry-go-round' train heading for Aberthaw power station. This train will shortly pass through the original GWR station at Aberdare that closed in 1964. When passenger services resumed in October 1988, the old up platform was resurfaced and a small ticket office built. The Welsh Assembly Government has requested Network Rail to provide a study for the possible extension of passenger services from Aberdare to Hirwaun.

In this photograph taken on Wednesday 10 April 2002, a loaded train of coal from Tower Colliery to Aberthaw power station led by 66 103 passes through the new Mountain Ash station. Passenger services over the original TVR line from Abercynon to Aberdare were withdrawn on 30 October 1964. The line reopened on 31 October 1988 although for some time before, special advertised passenger trains had run over the line on certain Saturdays. At first, the original Mountain Ash Oxford Street platform was used. However, on 29 January 2001, a brand-new station incorporating a passing loop, was opened on a new alignment. The original alignment is heading off to the left of the photograph alongside the fence. This area has always been prone to flooding by the River Cynon and new flood prevention work can be seen on the right.

On a sleepy August Sunday afternoon in the early 1980s, the driver and guard make their way along platform 2 of Barry Island station towards their train stabled in the carriage sidings. The class 116 DMUs will soon be heading back up the valleys carrying trippers who have spent the day on the beach and the funfair. The track bed in the centre originally led through the 280-yard tunnel to Barry Pier station where trains connected with steamer services to various places in the Bristol Channel on an "as required" basis. This line saw its last working in October 1971. The sidings have since been developed as a part of a Rail Heritage Centre.

On Friday 14 April 1995, an unidentified class 37 locomotive takes a train of fuel oil for Aberthaw power station across the 376-yard Porthkerry Viaduct. The viaduct, just to the west of Barry, had a very chequered early history. It was opened by the Vale of Glamorgan Railway, nominally independent but actually under the full control of the Barry Railway, on 1 December 1897. Just over a month after opening, on 10 January 1898, it had to be closed due to severe distortion of the eastern-most arches (to the right of the picture). This was attributed to inadequate foundations and poor quality workmanship. In order to keep the traffic running the Barry Railway built a $2\frac{1}{2}$ mile temporary line around the viaduct following the contours of the valley. Following a major reconstruction, the viaduct re-opened in January 1900 and has carried traffic without incident ever since.

In May 1997, Aberthaw power station held a public Open Day. Among the exhibits on show, were some examples of locomotives used to bring coal to the power station. As part of the activities, 60 037 was named *Aberthaw / Aberddawan*. In this photograph taken on the late afternoon of Sunday 25 May 1997, the recently named 60 037, furthest from the camera, leads 59 204 *Vale of Glamorgan*, 56 059 and 37 411 up the exit road from the power station into the yard at Aberthaw. From here the locos continued on to the stabling point next to Barry station, where they spent the night.

In the 1970s, the Ford Motor Company established a major engine works at Bridgend. As part of this development, a new branch line was built from Ford's Junction on the Vale of Glamorgan line into the factory site; this line was opened on 15 January 1980. In order to access the factory, the line had to cross the busy A48 road east of Bridgend and because of this, the branch is normally only used late at night or very early in the morning. In a rare daytime visit, an enthusiasts' special traversed the branch on Saturday 24 September 1994. 37 429 *Eisteddfod Genedlaethol* is seen nearer to the camera, with 37 158 in the distance as the train stands in the factory yard. The photograph is taken from the A48 Bridgend-Cowbridge road.

The combination of locomotives in EWS livery with crimson and cream coaching stock makes for a very rewarding picture. An enthusiasts' special, 'The Glamorgan Pioneer', a class 58 farewell tour, ran from Worksop to Swansea Burrows Yard and returned via Tondu. The train is seen here on Saturday 1 July 2000, approaching Miskin Loops on the South Wales main line and crossing the River Ely, as it returns from Swansea. At the front of the train is 58 037 *Worksop Depot* and 58 024. At the rear it is just possible to see 60 070 *John Loudon McAdam*.

In recent years several stations have opened on the South Wales main line between Bridgend and Cardiff. The latest of these was Llanharan in December 2007. This replaced the original station which closed in November 1964. On Saturday 28 March 2009, 66 128 is heading an eastbound train of steel coil from Margam steel works to Llanwern through the station. Like most new stations in the country, Llanharan is equipped with long approach ramps to access the platforms.

The line from Margam to Bridgend via Tondu provides a very useful diversion route when work has to be undertaken on the South Wales main line, even though it involves running round the train at Tondu. On Sunday 31 October 2004, the main line was closed and so 60 099 *Ben More Assynt* on a steel train from Margam had to take the diversion. Here it is seen coming off the Tondu branch at Llynfi Junction immediately to the west of Bridgend station and regaining the main line for its onward journey. The crossover in the foreground was installed in 1978 and provides the only access to the Vale of Glamorgan line from the west. Trains heading east for the Vale line have to run 'wrong line' through Bridgend Station.

Until the early 1980s, coal traffic in the Maesteg area remained buoyant. However, by 1985 only St. John's Colliery remained open. In the early summer of 1985, 37 294 is seen at Llynfi Junction, north of Maesteg, with coal from that colliery. The mine closed later that year on 2 November. Passenger services on the branch ceased in 1970, the last regular passenger service in South Wales to be withdrawn. The line was reopened to passenger traffic, as far as Maesteg, on 28 September 1992 with investment from Mid Glamorgan Council and the European Community. All the track shown in the photograph has now been lifted.

Following the end of coal mining in the valleys around Maesteg, large amounts of usable coal were stockpiled on land near Maesteg Washery. For several years, trains ran from here, carrying this coal away and, in August 1989, 37 691 stands at the stockpile site with a train of MDVs. To access the colliery, trains had to propel up a steep gradient and on a curve for a considerable distance from the old main line at the bottom of the valley. This had to be accomplished through what had become an unfenced area. For safety reasons, the train was accompanied by a shunter who acted as a lookout and was in contact by radio with the locomotive driver. These trains continued until services ceased on 13 October 1989.

The branch from Tondu to Pontycymmer in the Garw Valley was reopened in 1991 in order to remove large quantities of coal which had been reclaimed from tips north of Pontycymmer. The coal was taken direct to Aberthaw power station or to Neath Abbey Wharf for blending. Trains continued until 1997. On Thursday 20 February of that year, in the last week of operation, 56 113 takes empty wagons up the branch to a loading site just to the north of the old Pontycymmer station. Since its closure the line has remained dormant and now a local preservation group, the Garw Valley Railway, is actively pursuing its revival. They intend re-opening the line in stages south from Pontycymmer until it finally reaches Tondu.

In this photograph, taken from the now-demolished footbridge at the east end of Port Talbot station, two tanker trains head west. On the main line, runs 47 187 whilst 37 350 and 37 241 double-head their train on the down goods line. On the left of the picture which was taken on Friday 24 July 1992, track machines stand in the old Port Talbot Goods Yard. On the right of the picture is Port Talbot signal box which opened on 22 September 1963 with the introduction of Multiple Aspect Signalling to the area. It controls the South Wales main line as far as Llanharan to the east and Llanelli to the west.

On Friday 16 April 1999, a train headed by 66 021 is loading coal for Aberthaw power station in Johnson Brothers' Yard which lay immediately beyond the Steel Supply depot at Neath Abbey Wharf. It has just propelled the train under the bridge in the foreground, which carries the line from Dynevor Junction to Jersey Marine Junction South and then on to Swansea Burrows sidings which serve the docks. The further bridge carries the Swansea District line from Briton Ferry to Morlais Junction. The yard where the train is standing is now out of use for railway purposes.

In this photograph taken on Thursday 8 April 1993, 37 896 brings a loaded coal train from Coedbach, heading for Swansea Docks. The train is on the line between Jersey Marine North Junction and Jersey Marine South Junction. At the latter point, lines from the Vale of Neath and Dynevor Junction also join before the line heads down to Burrows yard for Swansea Docks. To the right of the picture is the single line from Jersey Marine South Junction to Neath and Brecon Junction and on to Onllwyn and Cwmgwrach. In the background can be seen the M4 motorway.

The line on the right of this picture is the former Vale of Neath Railway which opened in 1851. To the left is the former Neath and Brecon Railway which opened in 1864. They meet at Neath and Brecon Junction near the centre of the town of Neath. On Thursday 17 February 2005, 60 025 *Caledonian Paper* has been given the 'right-away' with an MGR train from Onllwyn to Immingham, while 66 030 awaits the road with the Serco test train which has just traversed the line up to Cwmgwrach. The loco on the rear of this train was 66 027.

In 1993, Ryan Mining opened a coal disposal point at Cwmgwrach in the Neath Valley. This was to serve small mines at Pentreclwydau, Lyn, Wenallt and Rheola. In order to achieve this, the Company received a £4.2 million Section 8 grant from the government. To access this facility the branch to Aberpergwm from Neath and Brecon Junction which had closed and been mothballed in 1985 was restored to use, and a new section north from there to Cwmgwrach was laid. On Wednesday 7 April 2004, 66 078 runs round its train at the north end of the Cwmgwrach facility. In 2007 the disposal point was mothballed and trains no longer run over the branch.

Onllwyn at the top of the Dulais Valley is a bleak place at the best of times, but a layer of fresh snow has given a Christmas card appearance to the area. On the morning of Monday 20 December 1999, 66 077 has arrived at the entrance to the washery and distribution centre, with a train of empty merry-go-round wagons for loading with coal from opencast sites in the area. It was running over two hours late due to frozen points at N & B Junction at Neath. Onllwyn station opened in June 1867 and closed in June 1964 and part of the old platform can be seen to the right of the locomotive. The run-round loop in use in this photograph has since been lifted and locomotives now run round inside the facility.

The privately-owned Marcroft Engineering Works situated near Burrows Sidings in Swansea, was a railway wagon repair centre. On Thursday 31 August 1995, class 09 105 has left the works which is just out of the picture on the right and is travelling along the overgrown track on its return to Burrows Sidings. The wagons which are stabled in the siding were there for many years. The track originally carried on curving around to the left towards Swansea Eastern Depot. The works closed in 1999 and 09 013 took out the last repaired wagons on 9 December of that year. The remaining wagons were removed by road and the works subsequently demolished.

In the early 1980s Swansea Docks retained much of the infrastructure of the steam age railway. Here, 08 592 is bringing a rake of wagons past King's Dock Junction signal box. The wagons are coming from the reception sidings near the dockside and will be propelled to coal hoists for the contents to be loaded onto a ship. The hoists can be seen in the background alongside the King's Dock. At this time much of the anthracite coal exported from Swansea went to Northern Ireland. The last working hoist in Swansea was taken out of use on 29 April 1987.

In the twenty-odd years that have elapsed since the previous photograph was taken, there have been huge changes at Swansea Docks. Virtually all the railway infrastructure has disappeared and only two lines remain in use in this photograph. Instead of coal being exported from Swansea it is now being brought in by ship. A large dump of recently unloaded coal can be seen on No. 4 Quay of the King's Dock. The date is Saturday 27 January 2001 and 66 144 is bringing in a train of empty wagons for filling with coal for Aberthaw power station. At the same time 08 995 *Kidwelly* is returning a train of empty wagons which were carrying steel billets from Margam steelworks for export by ship. These have been unloaded at No. 3 Quay ready for transfer to ship. In early 2010, only the line to No. 4 Quay is left and this has not seen use for some time.

The Swansea Avoiding Line, which runs from Landore Junction to Swansea Loop West Junction immediately to the north of Landore Traction Maintenance Depot, sees no regular freight traffic. This line, which is also known as the Swansea Loop, should not be confused with the Swansea District Line which lies several miles to the north. It provides a useful alternative route if the Swansea District Line cannot be used. In August 2004, the District Line was closed for track relaying and so on Wednesday 18 August, 60 043 (nearest the camera) and 60 034 top-and-tailed a Margam-Trostre steel train over the avoiding line. Two locomotives were needed because in order to enter Trostre tinplate works, the train had to reverse at Llandeilo Junction running into the up reception road and then over the Genwen Loop. Finally, it had to reverse again into the works sidings.

The viaduct which carries the Swansea to Llanelli line over the River Loughor is a remarkable structure. Originally built by Isambard Kingdom Brunel as part of the South Wales Railway in 1852, it is the only one of all the Brunel viaducts that still uses timber as part of its structure. The 235 yard viaduct still carries regular passenger trains, but only sees freight working when the Swansea District Line is closed. On Friday 20 August 2004, 60 043 (nearest the camera) at the front, and 66 085 at the rear, top-and-tail a Margam-Trostre steel train, diverted because of engineering work. A five-mile section of the line between Cockett and Dyffryn West near Llanelli, which included the viaduct, was singled in 1986. It is now planned to reinstate double track and the viaduct is the subject of a full review and survey for structural integrity.

Llandarcy Oil Refinery opened in 1921 and in its heyday sent several trains a day of refined petroleum products to many parts of Britain. By the 1990s its output was in decline and refining finished in 1999. On Saturday 24 September 1994, the site was visited by a Branch Line Society tour. 37 429 *Eisteddfod Genedlaethol* and 37 158 (nearest the camera) reverse off the Swansea District Line into the west end of the complex. On the left can be seen Llandarcy Ground Frame which was opened in 1920 as Lon Las South signal box. It was converted to a ground frame in February 1973. After the end of refining, some bitumen traffic remained but this ceased in 2009 and the whole complex is now being cleared.

The International Nickel Company (Mond) Ltd works at Clydach-on-Tawe was served by a short branch off the Swansea District Line at Felin Fran Junction. On Saturday 8 October 1983, the branch was visited by a Monmouthshire Railway Society tour. The class 117 DMU which formed part the train, is photographed at the entrance to the works having just passed under the extremely unstable-looking bridge which carries a local road. Would present Health & Safety regulations let anyone near this bridge today, let alone a train pass underneath? Not surprisingly, the bridge was subsequently demolished and replaced by a footbridge at a lower level. The Mond Works is still in production but no longer takes rail traffic and the track has been lifted. The embankments in the photograph are now heavily overgrown.

The 'Green Express' is an organisation committed to promoting public transport and sustainable tourism. On Monday 16 April 2001, they ran a train from Normanton to Cardiff via Warrington and 'The Heart of Wales Line'. It was hauled by 31 459 *Cerberus* and 31 190 *Gryphon* and is seen here passing Grovesend Colliery loop on the Swansea District Line. It has just travelled over the Hendy Loop which provides access from 'The Heart of Wales Line' at Pontarddulais to the Swansea District Line for eastbound trains. From the loop at the left of the picture, a line ran down to Brynlliw Colliery which was some distance behind the camera. This colliery opened in 1908 and closed in the 1920s. It was re-opened by the National Coal Board in 1961 and finally closed in 1982.

The 6-mile branch from Pantyffynnon to Gwaun-cae-Gurwen was mothballed in 1999 following the closure of opencast coal sites in the area. However, in 2009, Celtic Energy developed an opencast site near to the old colliery at East Pit. The cost of development of this site was over £4 million and some two million tons of coal is expected to be extracted over the next six to seven years. Driver training commenced in January 2009 and the first loaded coal train ran on the 28th of that month. This photograph was taken on Thursday 13 August 2009 and shows 66 176 crossing the River Amman north of Ammanford, with a loaded train of MEA wagons. The coal will be taken to Onllwyn for blending.

On Thursday 13 August 2009, 66 176 waits for the shunter to call it across Gwaun-cae-Gurwen Colliery crossing with a train of empty MEA wagons from Swansea Burrows yard. These will be filled at the Celtic Energy coal loading pad a few hundred yards further on. The modern attitude toward health and safety has brought a massive proliferation in the number of warning signs at level crossings. When you add to this the fact that they now have to be bilingual within Wales, you are left with what seems to be 'overkill'. However, in this strongly Welsh-speaking area such bilingualism is highly appropriate. One wonders how many steam locomotives will be seen at this point.

For a few years at the turn of the century, the daily Cardiff Central-Fishguard train was locomotive hauled, normally by a Class 37. The locomotive in charge of the train on Friday 16 August 2002, was 37 402 and this failed near Dynevor Junction on the Swansea District Line. Rescue did not arrive for some 2$\frac{1}{2}$ hours. Eventually 37 419 was attached to the rear of the train and propelled it to Llanelli where it was terminated and then returned 'empty stock' to Cardiff Canton. The photograph shows the driver of 37 419 leaning out of the cab as the train is propelled past Llandeilo Junction towards Llanelli station in the far distance. On the right of the picture can be seen Trostre tinplate works.

Llanelli stabling point was full of locomotives on Saturday 8 October 1983. From left to right, they were 03 120, 03 151, 03 144 and 08 649. The 03 locomotives were specially fitted with a cut-down cab and a headlight for working the Burry Port and Gwendraeth Valley Line and were also equipped for multiple working. The BPGV line had very limited clearances and the class 03s were the only locomotives allowed to travel over it to access Cwmmawr coal-loading facility. The line was closed and replaced by a newly refurbished connection between Coed Bach and Kidwelly in September 1983 and these locomotives then became redundant and were withdrawn from the line.

The 'Robeston Rumbler', a special train run by the Monmouthshire Railway Society, heads north out of Llanelli on the old Llanelli and Mynydd Mawr branch to Cynheidre Colliery. It is seen approaching Felin Foel No.2 level crossing just over 2 miles upline from the junction with the South Wales main line at Llanelli West. The date is Saturday 14 October 1989 and the colliery had closed some months previously. The tour train, a diesel multiple unit, was the last one to traverse the branch which has remained dormant ever since. However, The Llanelli and Mynydd Mawr Railway Company Limited, a heritage organisation has been active in recent years. The company has established a museum at Cynheidre and aims to reinstate rail services on the line north-eastwards from there towards Tumble.

Cwmmawr was a collection point for opencast coal from the Ffos Las opencast scheme and other smaller ones in the area. Coal was delivered here by lorry for loading into rail wagons. The line from here to Burry Port was originally built by the Burry Port and Gwendreath (sic) Valley Railway Company with restricted clearances and was liable to flooding, as parts of it were built on an old canal bed. In the early diesel locomotive era, only class 03 locomotives were allowed on the branch. In the 1980s, several class 08 locomotives were rebuilt with cut-down cabs for use between Cwmmawr and Coed Bach whilst the previously derelict line from Coed Bach to Kidwelly was refurbished to modern standards to replace the old BPGVR line which was then closed. On Thursday 31 August 1995, cut-down cab locomotive 08 995 *Kidwelly* shunts at Cwmmawr.

As mentioned in the caption to the previous photograph, the line from Coed Bach coal loading facility to Burry Port had a great many operational problems. To eliminate them, the original line from Kidwelly to the north-east side of Coed Bach, closed in the 1960s, was refurbished in September 1983. This meant that mainline locomotives could now reach the facility. On Thursday 11 April 1995, 56 053 *County of Mid Glamorgan/Sir Morgannwg Ganol* heads a train of coal, bound for export from Swansea Docks, down the new line. The Coed Bach facility can be seen in the left distance. The section of line from Cwmmawr to Coed Bach closed on 29 March 1996 and Coed Bach itself sent out its last train on 23 March 1998. All the buildings on both sites have subsequently been demolished.

In recent years the goods yard at Carmarthen has seen various activities. For a while, timber was loaded here and also there was some inward fertilizer traffic. Another short-term flow was the delivery of steel pipes and on Wednesday 18 April 2001, 66 025 stands in Carmarthen Goods Yard having just finished unloading sections of pipe which can be seen on the ground to the left of the crane. The train was split at Llandeilo Junction and run in two sections from there. A class 158 unit is leaving Carmarthen station with a train bound for West Wales via the west loop. The running line to the right of the train heads east towards Llanelli.

A class 153 single unit leaves Tenby station on Wednesday 17 August 1994, heading towards Whitland. Tenby is now the only passing point on the 16-mile branch from Whitland to Pembroke Dock. The loop is an unattended token exchange point since Tenby signal box closed on 10 December 1988. The station at Tenby was originally built by the Pembroke and Tenby Railway in 1863 as a terminus, before being extended to Whitland in 1866. It was built as standard gauge line at a time when the GWR through Whitland was broad gauge!

Clarbeston Road station which opened in 1854 is the junction for the Milford Haven and Fishguard Harbour lines. The station is 270 miles from Paddington via Gloucester. The signal box here was built in 1906 and is now the only one open in Pembrokeshire. In 1988 an NX (entrance/exit) panel was installed in it. The line to Milford Haven heads left in front of the box, whilst the Fishguard line goes straight ahead. On Friday 18 August 2006, 66 074 returns from Waterston, Milford Haven, to Machen Quarry with a train of empty stone wagons. The stone has been used in connection with the construction of liquefied natural gas holders.